Electric Vehicle Trip Log

by Richard Rosenthal

EV Model/Yr: ______________________________

Owned By: ______________________________

Odometer: ______________________________

Books by the author:

The Murder of Old Comrades

Sky Cops

K-9 Cops

Rookie Cop, Deep Undercover in the JDL (Jewish Defense League)

Practical Handgun Training

Self-Publishing~Simplified!

Nogales, Sasabe, Lochiel~ Part of our Third Nation

Use of Force in Modern Policing

Groundhog Day...

Electric Vehicles~What About Them?!?

Copyright © 2021 by Richard P. Rosenthal, Publisher

First Edition

This book is protected by copyright. No part of it may be reproduced in any manner without written permission from the publisher.

Available from: **Amazon**

Contact the author at: RichWellfleet@Comcast.net

Abbreviations

Too often I have seen explanations of the meaning of abbreviations used in books at the very end of the work. My thought is readers truly need them before starting on text containing unfamiliar material!

General/Common Terms

EV	Electric Vehicle
BEV	Battery Electric Vehicle (same type vehicle as an *EV*)
HEV	Hybrid Electric Vehicle (generally, a vehicle with no option to plug in for charging the on-board traction battery)
PHEV	Plug-in Hybrid Electric Vehicle
AC	Alternate Current
AFC	Alternate Fuel Vehicle (perhaps one using a biofuel)
DC	Direct Current (as used in an *EV* traction battery or drive battery)
DCFC	Direct Current Fast Charger. *DCFC* stations are springing up around the nation.
FCV	Fuel Cell Vehicle (most often hydrogen)
GOM	"Guess-O-Meter" (*EV* humor) or estimated mileage gauge
ICE	Internal Combustion Engine (a "normal" gasoline/diesel fuel auto)
NEMA	National Electrical Manufacturer Association. Most often seen in this book to describe electrical plug configurations (such as NEMA 14-50, or NEMA 5-20)
OEM	Original Equipment Manufacturer. Most often referring to auto manufacturers such as Ford, GM, VW, Tesla, etc.
SOC	State of Charge (of the traction battery)
ZEV	Zero Emission Vehicle (such as one using hydrogen for its fuel cell, or an *EV*)

Types of Charging "Plugs"

J1772	Common plug used in North and South America for "normal" *EV* charging.
CCS	Combined Charging System. Used for fast charging in the United States, Canada and Mexico. Most common for *EVs* here except for Tesla models (they use their own propriety configured plugs)
CHAdeMO	Seen in a few *EVs* in the United States. Used mostly in Europe, Japan and other Asian nations.
EVSE	Electric Vehicle Supply Equipment (an *EV's* "charger" unit. The "box" and cord attached from the electric outlet to your *EV*.)
SuperCharger	A term coined by Tesla for their fast charging plugs. These have the same basic plug configuration as their "normal" charge plug.
Tesla Destination Chargers	Level 2 chargers found at motels and restaurants for use by Tesla *EVs*.

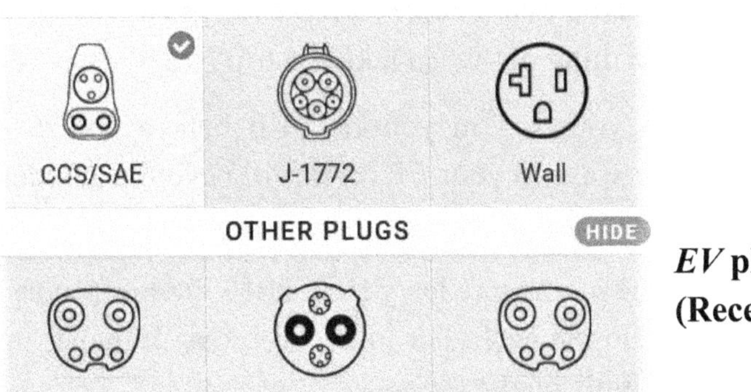

***EV* plug types (Receiving end)**

Purpose of this log

We (as in human society) are in a transition period, moving from the use of internal combustion engine (ICE) autos to electric vehicles (*EVs*). Those of you who are reading this preface already know that you (we, us, whoever) are the early adaptors. While it might not be a nutty, difficult and avantgarde "thing" to own an *EV* these days, neither is possessing an *EV* as simple as it might be if you were driving around in your "normal" gasoline powered Toyota Corolla.

Furthermore, I'm a bit of a nerd. Again, I suspect those reading these words would, to a lesser or greater degree, fall into the same category. Putting that thought in a more appropriate way, with more nuanced language, us "nerds" are curious about what's going on around us and seek to learn a bit more than the average person might want to know about any given subject. Our *EVs* are no exception.

For a while I tried making up my own "notebook" designed to contain useful relevant information I might wish to review in regard my *EV* trips. Problem was, I tended to lose the pages I'd created and found, in general, all I had done was create a bit of confusion for myself.

Thus the idea of this *EV* Trip Log.

Here is how I suggest you utilize this log:

- Keep a copy of it stored in your *EV*
- If you own more than one *EV*, keep a log in each
- Fill the darn thing out when taking a trip!

If you don't keep your log in your *EV* I'll bet ya you're gonna misplace it! If it's always in your *EV* there will never be any doubt as to where your trip log is at.

I have two *EVs* at the moment (Chevy Bolt, 2019 Premier, and a Tesla model Y). I keep a log in each. For logical reasons. It makes my life simpler and less complicated.

And this is the hard part; fill the thing out when charging up your *EV*! Don't' put it off. You'll forget, or you'll forget the particulars of the charging stop and eventually record the wrong information, defeating the whole purpose of the exercise.

As for the intentionally blank pages. Since most of us use ballpoint pens, and the pages of paperback books are pretty thin, if I didn't put a blank page on the opposite side of the page where you've scribbled your notes, and you kept on writing, you'd be hard pressed to decipher them later!

Happy *EVing* all!

Rich Rosenthal

Green Valley AZ/Cape Cod MA

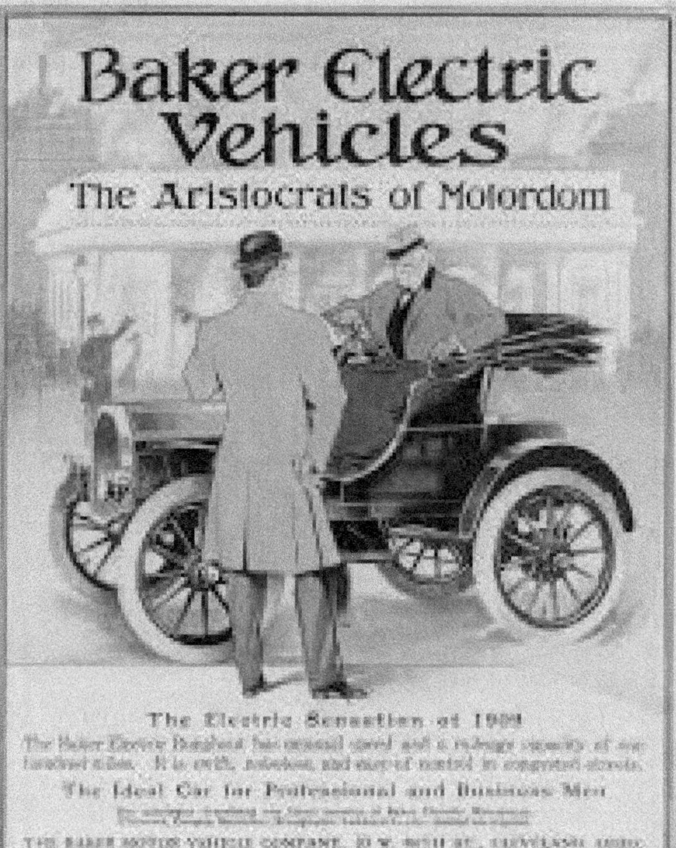
Baker Electric
Vehicles
The Aristocrats of Motordom
The Ideal Car for Professional and Business Men

EV Trip Log

Day/Date:____________ From/To:________________________

Odom Start/End:_______________ WX/Temp:________________

Notes for each stop:

DCFC/SC Location/Position Used: SOC Arrive/Leave: Charge Time:

____

____

____

____

____

____

____

____

____

____

Page Left Blank!

EV Trip Log

Day/Date:______________ From/To:___________________________

Odom Start/End:_________________ WX/Temp:_________________

Notes for each stop:

DCFC/SC Location/Position Used: SOC Arrive/Leave: Charge Time:

____

____

____

____

____

____

____

____

____

____

Page Left Blank!

EV Trip Log

Day/Date:____________ From/To:________________________

Odom Start/End:_______________ WX/Temp:________________

Notes for each stop:

DCFC/SC Location/Position Used: SOC Arrive/Leave: Charge Time:

____

____

____

____

____

____

____

____

____

____

Page Left Blank!

EV Trip Log

*Day/Date:*____________ *From/To:*________________________

*Odom Start/End:*_______________ *WX/Temp:*_______________

Notes for each stop:

DCFC/SC Location/Position Used: *SOC Arrive/Leave:* *Charge Time:*

____

____

____

____

____

____

____

____

____

____

Page Left Blank!

EV Trip Log

*Day/Date:*_____________ *From/To:*__________________________

*Odom Start/End:*________________ *WX/Temp:*_________________

Notes for each stop:

DCFC/SC Location/Position Used: *SOC Arrive/Leave:* *Charge Time:*

Page Left Blank!

EV Trip Log

*Day/Date:*____________ *From/To:*________________________

*Odom Start/End:*_______________ *WX/Temp:*_______________

Notes for each stop:

DCFC/SC Location/Position Used: *SOC Arrive/Leave:* *Charge Time:*

Page Left Blank!

EV Trip Log

*Day/Date:*____________ *From/To:*________________________

*Odom Start/End:*_______________ *WX/Temp:*________________

Notes for each stop:

<u>*DCFC/SC Location/Position Used:*</u> <u>*SOC Arrive/Leave:*</u> <u>*Charge Time:*</u>

____

____

____

____

____

____

____

____

____

____

Page Left Blank!

EV Trip Log

*Day/Date:*_____________ *From/To:*__________________________

*Odom Start/End:*________________ *WX/Temp:*_________________

Notes for each stop:

DCFC/SC Location/Position Used: *SOC Arrive/Leave:* *Charge Time:*

Page Left Blank!

EV Trip Log

*Day/Date:*_____________ *From/To:*__________________________

*Odom Start/End:*________________ *WX/Temp:*_________________

Notes for each stop:

DCFC/SC Location/Position Used: SOC Arrive/Leave: Charge Time:

Page Left Blank!

EV Trip Log

*Day/Date:*____________ *From/To:*________________________

*Odom Start/End:*_______________ *WX/Temp:*________________

Notes for each stop:

DCFC/SC Location/Position Used: *SOC Arrive/Leave:* *Charge Time:*

Page Left Blank!

EV Trip Log

Day/Date:______________ From/To:____________________________

Odom Start/End:__________________ WX/Temp:__________________

Notes for each stop:

DCFC/SC Location/Position Used: SOC Arrive/Leave: Charge Time:

Page Left Blank!

EV Trip Log

*Day/Date:*_____________ *From/To:*__________________________

*Odom Start/End:*________________ *WX/Temp:*_________________

Notes for each stop:

DCFC/SC Location/Position Used: *SOC Arrive/Leave:* *Charge Time:*

Page Left Blank!

EV Trip Log

Day/Date:____________ From/To:________________________

Odom Start/End:_______________ WX/Temp:________________

Notes for each stop:

DCFC/SC Location/Position Used: SOC Arrive/Leave: Charge Time:

____

____

____

____

____

____

____

____

____

____

Page Left Blank!

EV Trip Log

*Day/Date:*____________ *From/To:*________________________

*Odom Start/End:*_______________ *WX/Temp:*_______________

Notes for each stop:

DCFC/SC Location/Position Used: *SOC Arrive/Leave:* *Charge Time:*

Page Left Blank!

EV Trip Log

*Day/Date:*____________ *From/To:*________________________

*Odom Start/End:*_______________ *WX/Temp:*________________

Notes for each stop:

DCFC/SC Location/Position Used: *SOC Arrive/Leave:* *Charge Time:*

Page Left Blank!

EV Trip Log

*Day/Date:*____________ *From/To:*________________________

*Odom Start/End:*_______________ *WX/Temp:*_______________

Notes for each stop:

DCFC/SC Location/Position Used: *SOC Arrive/Leave:* *Charge Time:*

Page Left Blank!

EV Trip Log

*Day/Date:*____________ *From/To:*________________________

*Odom Start/End:*_______________ *WX/Temp:*________________

Notes for each stop:

DCFC/SC Location/Position Used: *SOC Arrive/Leave:* *Charge Time:*

Page Left Blank!

EV Trip Log

*Day/Date:*________________ *From/To:*____________________________

*Odom Start/End:*__________________ *WX/Temp:*__________________

Notes for each stop:

DCFC/SC Location/Position Used: *SOC Arrive/Leave:* *Charge Time:*

Page Left Blank!

EV Trip Log

*Day/Date:*_____________ *From/To:*___________________________

*Odom Start/End:*_________________ *WX/Temp:*__________________

Notes for each stop:

DCFC/SC Location/Position Used: *SOC Arrive/Leave:* *Charge Time:*

Page Left Blank!

EV Trip Log

*Day/Date:*____________ *From/To:*________________________

*Odom Start/End:*______________ *WX/Temp:*_______________

Notes for each stop:

DCFC/SC Location/Position Used: *SOC Arrive/Leave:* *Charge Time:*

Page Left Blank!

EV Trip Log

Day/Date:____________ From/To:________________________

Odom Start/End:_______________ WX/Temp:________________

Notes for each stop:

DCFC/SC Location/Position Used: *SOC Arrive/Leave:* *Charge Time:*

____

____

____

____

____

____

____

____

____

____

Page Left Blank!

EV Trip Log

*Day/Date:*____________ *From/To:*________________________

*Odom Start/End:*_______________ *WX/Temp:*_______________

Notes for each stop:

DCFC/SC Location/Position Used: SOC Arrive/Leave: Charge Time:

Page Left Blank!

EV Trip Log

*Day/Date:*______________ *From/To:*____________________________

*Odom Start/End:*_________________ *WX/Temp:*__________________

Notes for each stop:

DCFC/SC Location/Position Used: *SOC Arrive/Leave:* *Charge Time:*

Page Left Blank!

EV Trip Log

Day/Date:____________ From/To:________________________

Odom Start/End:_______________ WX/Temp:_______________

Notes for each stop:

DCFC/SC Location/Position Used: SOC Arrive/Leave: Charge Time:

Page Left Blank!

EV Trip Log

*Day/Date:*____________ *From/To:*________________________

*Odom Start/End:*_______________ *WX/Temp:*________________

Notes for each stop:

DCFC/SC Location/Position Used: *SOC Arrive/Leave:* *Charge Time:*

Page Left Blank!

EV Trip Log

*Day/Date:*______________ *From/To:*___________________________

*Odom Start/End:*_________________ *WX/Temp:*__________________

Notes for each stop:

DCFC/SC Location/Position Used: *SOC Arrive/Leave:* *Charge Time:*

Page Left Blank!

EV Trip Log

Day/Date:_____________ From/To:_________________________

Odom Start/End:________________ WX/Temp:________________

Notes for each stop:

DCFC/SC Location/Position Used: SOC Arrive/Leave: Charge Time:

____

____

____

____

____

____

____

____

____

____

Page Left Blank!

EV Trip Log

Day/Date:____________ From/To:________________________

Odom Start/End:_______________ WX/Temp:_______________

Notes for each stop:

DCFC/SC Location/Position Used: SOC Arrive/Leave: Charge Time:

____

____

____

____

____

____

____

____

____

____

Page Left Blank!

EV Trip Log

Day/Date:____________ From/To:________________________

Odom Start/End:_______________ WX/Temp:________________

Notes for each stop:

DCFC/SC Location/Position Used: SOC Arrive/Leave: Charge Time:

____

____

____

____

____

____

____

____

____

____

Page Left Blank!

EV Trip Log

Day/Date:_____________ From/To:__________________________

Odom Start/End:________________ WX/Temp:_________________

Notes for each stop:

DCFC/SC Location/Position Used: *SOC Arrive/Leave:* *Charge Time:*

Page Left Blank!

EV Trip Log

*Day/Date:*_____________ *From/To:*___________________________

*Odom Start/End:*________________ *WX/Temp:*_________________

Notes for each stop:

<u>*DCFC/SC Location/Position Used:*</u> <u>*SOC Arrive/Leave:*</u> <u>*Charge Time:*</u>

Page Left Blank!

EV Trip Log

Day/Date:____________ From/To:________________________

Odom Start/End:_______________ WX/Temp:________________

Notes for each stop:

DCFC/SC Location/Position Used: SOC Arrive/Leave: Charge Time:

____

____

____

____

____

____

____

____

____

____

Page Left Blank!

EV Trip Log

*Day/Date:*______________ *From/To:*___________________________

*Odom Start/End:*_________________ *WX/Temp:*__________________

Notes for each stop:

DCFC/SC Location/Position Used: SOC Arrive/Leave: Charge Time:

Page Left Blank!

EV Trip Log

Day/Date:____________ From/To:________________________

Odom Start/End:_______________ WX/Temp:________________

Notes for each stop:

<u>DCFC/SC Location/Position Used:</u> <u>SOC Arrive/Leave:</u> <u>Charge Time:</u>

____

____

____

____

____

____

____

____

____

____

Page Left Blank!

EV Trip Log

Day/Date:____________ From/To:________________________

Odom Start/End:_______________ WX/Temp:________________

Notes for each stop:

DCFC/SC Location/Position Used: SOC Arrive/Leave: Charge Time:

Page Left Blank!

EV Trip Log

*Day/Date:*____________ *From/To:*________________________

*Odom Start/End:*_______________ *WX/Temp:*________________

Notes for each stop:

DCFC/SC Location/Position Used: *SOC Arrive/Leave:* *Charge Time:*

____

____

____

____

____

____

____

____

____

____

Page Left Blank!

EV Trip Log

*Day/Date:*____________ *From/To:*________________________

*Odom Start/End:*_______________ *WX/Temp:*________________

Notes for each stop:

DCFC/SC Location/Position Used: *SOC Arrive/Leave:* *Charge Time:*

Page Left Blank!

EV Trip Log

Day/Date:____________ From/To:________________________

Odom Start/End:_______________ WX/Temp:_______________

Notes for each stop:

DCFC/SC Location/Position Used: SOC Arrive/Leave: Charge Time:

____

____

____

____

____

____

____

____

____

____

Page Left Blank!

EV Trip Log

*Day/Date:*____________ *From/To:*________________________

*Odom Start/End:*_______________ *WX/Temp:*_______________

Notes for each stop:

DCFC/SC Location/Position Used: SOC Arrive/Leave: Charge Time:

Page Left Blank!

EV Trip Log

Day/Date:____________ From/To:________________________

Odom Start/End:_______________ WX/Temp:________________

Notes for each stop:

DCFC/SC Location/Position Used: SOC Arrive/Leave: Charge Time:

____

____

____

____

____

____

____

____

____

____

Page Left Blank!

EV Trip Log

*Day/Date:*____________ *From/To:*________________________

*Odom Start/End:*______________ *WX/Temp:*_______________

Notes for each stop:

DCFC/SC Location/Position Used: *SOC Arrive/Leave:* *Charge Time:*

Page Left Blank!

EV Trip Log

Day/Date:____________ From/To:________________________

Odom Start/End:_______________ WX/Temp:________________

Notes for each stop:

DCFC/SC Location/Position Used: SOC Arrive/Leave: Charge Time:

Page Left Blank!

EV Trip Log

Day/Date:____________ From/To:________________________

Odom Start/End:_______________ WX/Temp:________________

Notes for each stop:

DCFC/SC Location/Position Used: SOC Arrive/Leave: Charge Time:

____

____

____

____

____

____

____

____

____

____

Page Left Blank!

EV Trip Log

*Day/Date:*____________ *From/To:*________________________

*Odom Start/End:*_______________ *WX/Temp:*_______________

Notes for each stop:

DCFC/SC Location/Position Used: SOC Arrive/Leave: Charge Time:

Page Left Blank!

EV Trip Log

Day/Date:____________ From/To:________________________

Odom Start/End:_______________ WX/Temp:_______________

Notes for each stop:

DCFC/SC Location/Position Used: SOC Arrive/Leave: Charge Time:

Page Left Blank!

www.ingramcontent.com/pod-product-compliance
Lightning Source LLC
LaVergne TN
LVHW010453160826
845677LV00012B/2460

* 9 7 9 8 7 1 7 3 4 6 7 9 5 *